THINK!

A LOOK AT OUR CHILDREN'S DAYS AT SCHOOL

By Cormac O'Brolcháin, CSSp, PhD

Illustrated by
Padraic O'Brolcháin

ORIGINAL WRITING

© 2009 Cormac O'Brolcháin

Designed by Mella O'Brolchain

978-1-907179-00-6

A CIP catalogue for this book is available from the National Library.

Published by Original Writing Ltd., Dublin, 2009.

Printed by Cahills of Dublin.

This short work is dedicated to
the families and teachers of Ireland

My deepest thanks to all those who helped to bring
this work to fruition, especially my brother Padraic, my niece Mella,
Caroline Mullan and my fellow Spiritans, Tom Nash, John Kevin,
Jim McDonnell and Brian Gogan.

Contents

Introduction 7

Chapter 1: On the way 9

Chapter 2: At school – part 1 17

Chapter 3: At school – part 2 25

Chapter 4: Our children 35

Chapter 5: Our children's gifts 39

Chapter 6: Intelligence 45

Chapter 7: EQ and SQ 53

Chapter 8: Choosing a school 59

Chapter 9: 'Something else?' 67

Chapter 10: Back home 75

References 80

Introduction

Our children are special and they are great. They are miracles in their own right. They make life, our lives, so hopeful and so wonderful. Yes, like ourselves, they have problem days with their ups and downs, but life without them is unimaginable. Besides one's spouse or 'better-half', children are the greatest treasure parents can have. So, bearing this in mind, this short book considers the school days of these price-less gifts, our children – those days that pass so quickly and yet have a profound influence on their lives. The object of this book is merely to share some thoughts about a normal school day. There is no attempt to address holiday time, just the routine of school days.

In summary, the book talks about a typical day during all those fleet-ing years when our children wake up and, with or without some morning sustenance, prepare to go to school. They pack their bags, their sports gear, some food and various other items when needed; occasionally some very young ones pack teddy bears or items that will remind them of home.

After saying goodbye to home they wend their way on foot, on bicycle, bus, train or car to school, sometimes accompanied, some-times not. Arriving at school, they strive to settle down to spend their day 'mostly studying', with some little 'break time' built in. Many children like school. Others, however, find it very hard to settle down or to accept the 'school thing' at all. A number of children just put up with it.

After six to eight hours they once again pack their belongings and wend their way home again; normally with them will travel further instructions for continued work at home. Arriving home, often quite tired, they begin their designated 'homework' and, after eating some food, they prepare for bed. Some have time for relaxation, but soon it is time for bed and the rest needed in preparation for the morrow when the gainfully occupying school will start all over again.

One day, however, after years of this lifestyle, our children will wake up and find that they are no longer school children.

What now? Are they ready for the next stage of their journey? Has their school prepared them well? What do they really hope for out of life and who and what do they truly love? What will they work hard to achieve and who do they think they are in their inner selves? Will they thank us for sending them to school or to the schools we sent them to for all those years?

I have seen parents with tears in their eyes as their children graduate from secondary school. "It seems only like yesterday when they joined the school; where did the years go?" "This is the last of our three children, doesn't life pass so quickly?"

Interestingly, very few ask whether school was or is a good idea. So I feel it is worth our while spending some short time considering each aspect of our child's normal school day.

Enjoy!

Chapter 1: On the Way

The night has passed and our children have put on their school uniforms, if such is required, in preparation for the school day. Will they leave for school with a bounce in their step? Happily, many do but unfortunately others do not.

1. 'Bags'

Recently, a child in junior infants, barely five years of age, arrived at school with 'bags' under his eyes. I asked him if he had been up late the previous night. He reluctantly nodded and agreed, glumly admitting, "I am a TV addict." Another child, lethargic and sad, explained that she didn't sleep much since her dad and mum were fighting again –"And I couldn't stop them." Another explains with a tear in his eye, "My grandad is dying". Many young children carry problems to school.

Others, generally teenagers, sometimes find Mondays difficult having spent the weekend with little sleep and too much 'celebration'. Some reduce the working week to four days or sometimes less.

2. Bags

Talking of bags, what loads our children carry on their way to school! The sight of school children weighed down with school bags bulging at the seams is surely distressing. Are such loads really necessary?

I have seen children carrying not merely one bag but three bags. With such loads can their backs remain healthy? One day a child travelled to school on a bicycle with two heavy bags 'aboard'. When he fell, being unable to keep his balance with the heavy bags, he was almost decapitated by a passing van. It was a lucky escape; the bicycle was a write-off.

In a bus an elderly woman preparing to get off at her stop was hit by a swinging schoolbag and fell to the floor. The bag was full with the day's required load. The child who was carrying the bag on his shoulder had turned to talk to his travelling companion without noticing the woman.

In an interview on CBS, the paediatric orthopaedic surgeon Dr Michael Vitale, speaking on The Early Show to consumer correspondent Susan Koeppen, said "We're really seeing an epidemic of back pain in children these days". He explained that he saw children every day with back pain. It was pointed out that in the previous year nearly 4,000 children went to the emergency room because of back-pack injuries. Dr Vitale went on to say that "Kids often have significant back pain that limits their activities, limits their ability to play sports and interact with peers, and it can't be a good thing to start having back pain at the age of 5 or 6".

How children carry their bag may also cause the strain, Dr Vitale explained. When more than half the schoolbag is below the waist it creates an unnatural force on the lower back. Also, when the schoolbag is only around one shoulder, all that weight is really on a small set of muscles just on one side.

The following recommendations were made:

+ A bag of the right size.
+ Make sure it fits and is worn high; a waist strap also helps.
+ Straps should be wide and padded and make sure the child uses both straps.

- Consider a bag with wheels although the child may still have to lift it in and out of cars, train or bus.

The American Physical Therapy Association, American Academy of Orthopaedic Surgeons and American Chiropractic Association have made the following specific recommendations regarding weight limits on the basis that the acceptable load in a backpack is related to a child's weight:

- A 60 lb child can carry a maximum backpack weight of 5 lbs
- 60-75 lb child can carry 10 lbs
- 100 lb child can carry 15 lbs
- 125 lb child can carry 18 lbs
- 150 lb child can carry 20 lbs
- 200 lb child can carry 25 lbs.

It was then suggested that this might be achieved if the children

- Keep a second set of heavy textbooks at home where possible.
- Can use handouts instead of textbooks for homework.
- Can use separate bags for separate activities and don't need to carry athletic or after school gear while in class.

England and France have also considered these problems. According to BackCare (www.backcare.org.uk), a charity for healthier backs in the UK, back pain affects over one third of the adult population in the UK. Also:

- The National Health Service (2007) announced that it spends more than £1 billion on back pain related costs per year.
- The Health and Safety Executive estimates that musculoskeletal disorders, which includes back pain, costs UK employers between £590 million and £624 million per year.

- In England it transpires therefore that the total cost of back pain corresponds to between 1% and 2% of gross national product (GDP).

Can we parents and teachers, then, do anything about the daily load of our children besides following the recommendations above? I feel we can. Parents and teachers on boards of management and school committees might consider whether weight could be an issue when choosing schoolbooks. A study could be made of our schools' timetables so that on a given day unnecessary books could remain at home. Those drawing up timetables might take into account the weight of books so that not all the heavy books would be needed on any one day. Further, we could ask our schools for safe storage in the school so that the carrying of many books to and from school would not always be necessary.

And does this apply equally to boys and girls? Most studies have found that back pain is more common in girls; and unfortunately genes also can be part of the problem, as there seems to be an association between non-specific low back pain in parents and their offspring. One way or another, we need to give this aspect of schooling time and thought.

3. 'On Their Way'

So on their way to school they go. Some go alone, some walk, some cycle; some go by bus or train. Some are brought to school by car or by special buses. What do they hear and what do they see or experience on the way?

I recently took a trip on the local train. Having decided not to read the litany of mini, minor and major 'disasters' on the pages of the newspapers I instead observed the world around me in the train and through the window. It was a most educational venture. The advertisements shouting for attention and pushing out the boundaries with their subliminal messages, the graffiti on the walls and on the houses or on wherever was available, the communications through numerous foreign languages, the loud sharing of mobile phone conversations, the postures of those who came and went, the dress codes, the hair colours and styles, the banter and the 'slagging' – all told me how different the world has become in such a short time. "Is it true," one child asked, "that when you were young you had to know where a person was before you phoned her?" Another child asked: "Were drugs not peddled on the buses and trains when you were going to school?"

On their way to school our children can enjoy themselves and be unharmed and be safe. On the other hand they could experience much that is negative. They could be called names; they could hear rumours or false stories about themselves; they could hear others telling their friends not to be friends with them any more; they could be beaten or kicked or pushed or hassled about how they look, about their weight, their religion, their colour, their medical condition, their disability, their failure or their 'nerdy' success in studies. Their property also can be stolen or hidden. They can receive demands for their money or property. Jokes about them can be spread or threats and suggestions of nasty happenings that could befall them. Homophobic remarks can be thrown at them. They can be the subject of horseplay, especially when they do not like it.

The following signs/symptoms may suggest that our children are being hassled: anxiety about travelling to and from school; unwillingness to go to school at all; playing truant; deterioration in their school work; unexplained illness; changes in mood or behaviour; signs of anxiety such as sleep disorder; crying and bedwetting. Our children can also come out with remarks about fellow students or teachers that are not in character. Evidently, if their possessions are damaged or gone missing or our child steals from home or makes more than normal requests for money, these too could suggest a problem. Signs of bruising or damaged clothing and refusal to discuss the problem are obvious danger signals. In brief, if any of the signs/symptoms above continue, our child very probably needs help.

4. Mobile Phones

The advantages of mobile phones are legion. Our children can easily contact their parents and parents can readily contact their children. In extreme cases our children's whereabouts can be ascertained through the signal from their phones; and the sophistication of phones is increasing by the month. Our children can also share their experiences in a visual fashion and many parents will soon be able to talk face-to-face with their children at any time. It can also give a feeling of security. However, there are other sides to mobile phones.

Mobile phones increasingly are becoming a weapon of choice for bullies. Many pay-as-you-go mobile phones can be bought over the counter and do not require proof of identity, so that calls made from them can be almost untraceable. In the findings of John Carr, a technology adviser for the NCH* in England, "For a child or teenager being bullied by mobile phone, it can be terrifying and feel like there is no escape." His research suggests that mobile phones, particularly with cameras, are being used by bullies to frighten and intimidate others. The NCH surveyed 770 youngsters and found 14% of 11 to 19-year-olds had been threatened or harassed using text messages and bullies had used images taken with mobile phone cameras to intimidate or embarrass one in ten young people. This included singling out overweight or 'spotty' youngsters and recording and sharing acts of playground violence. The findings follow reports of so-called

*NCH — National Children's Homes (Action for Children)

'happy slapping' attacks - where assaults on children and adults are recorded on mobile phones and sent via video messaging. Musician Myleene Klass, who helped launch a support website to address this problem, said that text messaging was a language almost exclusive to children. "To kids, it's a language that they use every single day, and now it's becoming a bullying tool," she said.

Happily, parents can deal with this situation if they contact the mobile phone network the child is using and tell them what is happening.

5. "Plugged In"

We have all seen children with earphones in their ears, "plugged in" to what could be described as a parallel world. This 24/7 world of pop music is worth taking a brief look at. Although the music is hidden in discs and iPods and now-rare cassettes, it pulsates with meaning and messages. The rhythms of the drums and bass guitars, the melodies, the words expressing various emotions, all usually readily understood, fill our children's minds and hearts. While there are indeed many beautiful and inspiring lyrics and songs in today's pop music, there are also those that are not.

It might be worthwhile for us parents and teachers to listen to this music, read the words of the lyrics and evaluate the values being passed on to our children. We will discuss 'pop' music later.

Chapter 2: At School - Part 1

When our children finally arrive at school, they are expected to put away their iPods, disc and cassette players and their phones. The world they have just visited is expected to be put on hold. It is not always easy to achieve this; some children do attempt to keep in contact with their other world throughout the day and sometimes try to send messages, snapshots and short video recordings to 'elsewhere'.

1. Welcome

So, as they enter the school buildings, we might ask ourselves whether our children feel happy and are at home there or do they enter feeling lonely and out of place? In this regard, the importance of having a caring and benign secretary, particularly in primary schools, can hardly be overstated. The ambience and 'welcome' at the entrance to the school is most important.

I spoke to a well-known architect who had designed a splendid hotel in a holiday resort in Africa. Africa has so many wonderful and exotic resorts. However, the architect explained to me that while the hotel had to give a flavour of Africa, his remit was to design a foyer where the visitors would feel 'at home'.

I remember a little child in the tropics who was a boarder in a school. He was just seven. When the children woke up one morning the little boy was gone. Pandemonium ensued. Having thoroughly searched everywhere, it was found that the boy was definitely missing. Just as the police were about to be informed, a car arrived in the school and out stepped the boy with his teddy bear in hand. He had been found over a mile from the school. When the driver of the car who picked him up asked the child where he was going, he resolutely replied: "I am going home to my mum and dad."

Even buses and cars that ferry young children to school can affect them. One mother who was on 'her week' ferrying a local group of young children to school found that the children did not want to go with her. It transpired that the children had no problem with the mother who was indeed upset, but the 'ugly' design of the car she drove for some reason made the very young children afraid. It is said that chickens, although they may never have seen a hawk, run for cover when even its shadow appears.

2. Hot and Cold

Imagine us adults arriving in the foyer of the buildings where we work and realise that there is no central heating for cold days, no proper ventilation for hot days and draughts abound.

So, what about our children? It is so important that we make sure that the overall school buildings our children daily attend are properly heated, properly insulated and have adequate fresh air.

I remember being in a school where the children had to wear gloves and coats in the school; it was bitterly cold. It is so difficult to work when we are too cold – and evidently it is most difficult to write while wearing gloves. In one school the teachers who found their school too cold took the initiative and refused to teach. Obviously heating systems do break down but only a limited amount of cold can be withstood if work is to continue.

The same applies to heat; children cannot work when it is too hot. I have seen children agitated and perspiring copiously in classrooms that were too hot for them. In Ireland this heat problem is rare but it can apply when there is lack of air in classrooms on the rare hot day and the children begin falling asleep and cannot concentrate.

3. Water and Wet Days

Water is so important for us humans. In hotter climes it is often the presence or absence of rain and water supplies that closes schools. I was in a school where the normal hot weather persisted but the water supply failed. It was acceptable for one day but then the school had to close. Each day very considerable amounts of water are needed in all schools, especially in toilets, whatever the climate.

Then there are those very wet days. Can our children change their clothes if they arrive at school soaking wet? Are there facilities for drying their clothes? One young girl, while playing in a school-yard, fell into a rather large pool of water. She was drenched to the bone. The school had no means of dealing with the situation. Even appealing to home was no good since there was no one at home. Finally, an electric fire was found that dried both the tears and the clothes of the child.

But, even if our children arrive in school dry, they may end up play-ing during recreation and be caught in a torrential downpour. What then? In our various places of work we might not appreciate the vaga-ries of the weather if we are involved indoors away from the elements, whereas our children could well be right in the middle of it all.

Another problem with wet days is that during break times the chil-dren have to be kept in. This can be most problematic. Children, our 'bundles of energy', need time and space to let off steam, to flex their muscles, move, jump and run. Ideally there should be space inside the school buildings for when it is wet and outside the school buildings when it is sufficiently dry, to allow for this need. Children, like adults, often reflect the weather. They become depressed in bad weather and this is exacerbated when they cannot exercise. It is definitely easier to teach when the sun is shining, provided it is not too hot.

4. Place for Storage

Again, imagine adults arriving in their work place to find there is little or no room to hang their coats, no place for safely storing their bags or other personal items. Our children can have the same issues facing them.

Is there locker space for our children to store their books, their sporting gear and so on? So many times I have seen piles of bags, along with coats, lunch boxes, musical instruments, games outfits and equipment, lying in corridors; so much space is needed. It is a joy to see children bringing all sorts of paraphernalia to school showing that they are fully involved in the curricular and extra-curricular provisions of the school. But it is sad, when due to lack of space, their belongings are put at risk of damage or theft. "Someone has broken my tennis racquet!" "My guitar and loudspeaker are gone!" "My football is missing!" Very often the children have just mislaid their belongings but the risk of damage or theft still remains.

One day two visitors, a man and a woman, came into a school. It appeared evident that they were parents either looking for the Principal or one of the teachers. They seemed to be well known in the school, smiling and saluting various teachers, though no one was called by name. It was only when they quickly disappeared that questions were asked and, following an inspection, various items were found to be missing. It transpired that each teacher thought that other teachers knew these 'visitors' when in fact no one did. "My bag is gone!"

Another day a lorry arrived 'to make a delivery to a school'. It stopped and the driver and the person travelling with the driver got out. In a very few minutes many of the bicycles in the bicycle rack were on their way into the back of the lorry, each lock having been briskly broken.

Happily the foul deed was observed and the lorry load was prevented from leaving the school; all bicycles were retrieved. But thefts do occur in schools and can be perpetrated by both outsiders and insiders.

6. Toilets

What of the toilets in our offices and work places? What about those provided for our children? One Principal of a school recently suggested that the quality of a school could be measured by the condition of its toilets. Are our children provided with well-maintained and clean toilets along with adequate toilet paper, soap and drying facilities? Or do they find broken locks and seats, non-functioning flushing mechanisms, no soap, dodgy taps, dirty towels or malfunctioning hand-drying machines, not to mention prurient graffiti reminding them of the world they have put on hold?

I remember visiting one school during the holidays. In the toilet area most of the locks on the doors were broken, some doors had holes in them, which were generally stuffed with toilet paper, and various 'messages' were written or drawn inside the cubicles on walls and doors. This, evidently, happens in many public amenities, but we should make sure it does not happen where our children are being educated.

I also imagine most parents would hope that in their children's schools, unlike the vast majority of toilets in public places, there are no vending machines with safe and extra safe condoms, peppermints and chewing gum.

I remember visiting a small picturesque town in rural Ireland that had only two shops/pubs and a few houses. For interest, I visited the toilets of both premises to find out if such vending machines were in place; they were. Will our schools in time, after various government debates and EU decisions regarding the age of consent and 'safe sex', recommend or insist on them being in our schools?

7. Corridors

What about the corridors our children use? Are the walls of the corridors bare or decorated, impersonal or warm? What symbols, if any, are there on the walls and what meanings do they carry for our children? For example, if there are crosses on the walls, what are they like? Do they remind our children of Calvary or merely cross-bedecked pop singers?

If there are paintings or artefacts, do the children resonate with them? Is the children's artwork and craftwork displayed? Are there photographs on the walls? If there are, are they of teams or of individuals? Are they of the past or of the present? What does their display suggest? I remember walking along the corridors of one school and the footballers had pride of place. In another, portraits of 'successful' past students bedecked the walls. In another, gaudy posters covered the walls along with handwritten notices. Each school was saying something to the children, either deliberately or unwittingly.

Along the corridors of some schools flowers decorate the windowsills; in other schools there are none. One Principal suggested that flowers be put in place in the windowsills of the school where he worked but was strongly advised that they would be vandalised in a very short time. Despite the warning, the Principal decided to go ahead and implement the plan. The flowers are still blooming many years later.

Vending machines with soft drinks, sweets and chocolate bars are sometimes permitted on corridors. Certainly they are good money-spinners, but I wonder if they promote healthy eating habits or promote good educational values?

8. Width of Corridors

What about the width of the corridors in the schools where our children attend? To be able to walk down corridors that promote a feeling of community life, be they in schools, offices or public build-ings is far too rare. Spacious corridors make such a difference by affording those who use them room to stop, to talk and to relate. In narrow corridors we normally are forced to keep moving lest we block others. Humans, I feel, do not flourish in narrow spaces.

I visited four schools recently. In the first school there were wide corridors and they were filled with groups of students walking, talking, laughing and relating to one another. There seemed to be a very happy spirit there. In the second and third schools, however, which were newly built secondary schools, the corridors were narrow and only one-way traffic was permitted. In the fourth school, while visiting with a school team, I found myself walking sideways with a sports bag since the corridor was not sufficiently wide to allow a 70k person with a sports bag fit between the two walls. Had the school boards passed the plans for these corridors?

It is true that if a school is already built there is little one can do about the width of corridors. It is also true that wide corridors cost money but, since generations of children will pass through school corridors, it would seem important to give them a chance to be able to walk with others, rather than in single file while being forced to talk over their shoulders. School is not a preparation for life, it is life, and for some children their time at school will be the largest part of their lives; in the rare case it will be their only life.

9. Their Own Space

When we adults attend conferences we would normally expect the conference rooms to be sufficiently large to allow adequate personal space for each one attending. I imagine if we were continually cramped into small rooms we would be fairly unhappy and do something about it. So, what kind of classrooms do our children inhabit when they attend school? Are the classrooms airy and roomy or are they cluttered and almost full even when the children are not in them? I have studied both long-established and newly built schools. Often the space afforded our children, even in the newer buildings, is quite inadequate.

In one classroom, built in accordance with government regulations and in the recent past, twenty-five students were 'cribbed, cramped and confined' into such an inadequate space that some pupils' desks were flush with that of the teacher in order to fit in. In a computer room in the same school, the computers had to be placed in circles in order to fit into the room; this arrangement left about thirty-percent of the children out of the teacher's line of sight. To be faced occasionally with such problems might be tolerated but on a day-to-day basis such 'educational spaces' are surely unacceptable.

Chapter 3: At School – Part 2

One night, while visiting a house at the equator and having retired for the night in a heavy blanket of heat, I noticed after a few minutes that all the lorries travelling to the city seemingly had to pass our house just outside the gate. At the gate the lorries turned a corner and changed gears. On and on, an endless line of lorries passed every three to four minutes. Coping with the noise was quite difficult but in due course some immunity was built up. But, just as immunity to the noise of the lorries was built up, another noise pattern entered my consciousness – a twenty-four hour blanket-making factory just across the road. The machinery in the factory seemed to operate with a triple thump mechanism; each cycle consisting of three thumps. Whereas the first was soft or *mezzo piano* and the second merely *mezzo forte*, the final thump was a significantly terrible, '*sforzando*'. When this third thump had struck, the process began again and again and again. And that wasn't the end. Having struggled to set up immunity to the thumps, I noticed a high-pitched buzzing at my ears; evidently the resident army of mosquitoes had decided to come out in force. Though the bed was covered with a mosquito net, the army seemed only inches away from my ears and face. Sad to say, at 4am I decided that the night of no sleep was over and, packing my bag, I turned on the light and waited for dawn.

1. Noise?

What about noise then? Do our children go to schools that are in quiet areas or are they spending their school days in the midst of the noise of industry, city-life or airports? If it is the latter, is there adequate soundproofing in place so that our children can spend their days in classrooms cut off from the noise, allowing them to be reasonably relaxed and adequately able to concentrate on what is happening in the classroom? Children are quite docile and if the classrooms they attend are being subjected to constant noise they might just put up with it, knowing no better.

For some years I was on the staff of a school in the tropics. There was a very noisy building project in progress nearby. For about one year the constant noise of the machines employed there enabled the children to talk to each other without readily being detected by their teachers. The children, despite the noise, were unperturbed and quite happy; but no one was surprised when the school achieved relatively poor results in that year's public examinations. A quiet environment, in my view, is an educational must, though there are others with different views.

One American visitor from a bustling noisy city visited a quiet village deep in the Irish countryside. During the day she found the town quaint and peaceful with only the rare motorbike or car breaking the silence, but at night when she went to bed she found she couldn't sleep. When the owner of the house heard a noise in the kitchen late into the night he went downstairs and found his visitor; she was asleep beside the humming fridge. Maybe we can adapt to noise?

Also, some children in Africa who attended a boarding school in Nairobi had a somewhat similar problem. They found it very hard to sleep at night unless they had conch shells at their ears. When asked what they were doing, they explained that they lived beside the Indian Ocean where there was a reef with waves breaking all day and night. Without that noise, they explained, they did not feel at home.

2. Ventilation

Parents know what lack of ventilation means in houses, offices and work places so we might ask whether there is sufficient ventilation in our children's classrooms. When a group of twenty-plus children sit hour after hour in a room, good ventilation is so important. Without sufficient ventilation the group can feel sleepy and underachieve.

In one school hall, being used as a centre for government examinations, a supervisor observed that the heads of some examinees were beginning to droop. It was a hot day, the hall was full, it was afternoon and the sun was shining directly in through the windows. Happily, the supervisor was proactive and used common sense so the situation was duly rectified; he opened the windows. Unfortunately such common sense may not be so common.

In some schools in warm weather classroom doors are kept open so that the children can have the fresh air they need to concentrate. I have frequently seen this 'open-door policy'. In a school in the tropics where I spent some years there were doors on both sides of the classrooms. These doors were kept open to allow for a flow of air; the heat was normally ninety degrees Fahrenheit. But not far from the school was the noisy central street of the city; it was a delicate balance. Proper ventilation is a challenge to architects and most important for our children in school.

3. Draughts and Leaks

In damp cold weather are our children's classrooms dry and pleasant or do they leak and allow in draughts? I observed in one school a series of pots in a classroom, placed seemingly randomly on the floor, only to realise that they were precisely placed to collect the drips from the leaking roof. In another, I wondered where the draught was coming from only to be shown that there was no windowpane; it had been broken and not replaced. Windows can be badly fitted, doors can have large gaps underneath or at the sides and high ceilings can also cause problems; all these can make it very difficult to keep classrooms warm and dry, while both heating and maintenance are expensive.

4. Light

What about light in the classrooms? Is natural light used or is there need for artificial light? I remember one study hall that did not have sufficient natural light so artificial light was used. It seemed adequate but within a year a number of those who studied there ended up wearing glasses. On investigation, it was concluded that the lack of adequate lighting was the root cause.

But too much light is also a hazard and the question must be asked as to whether the sun shines though the classroom windows in a benign way or does it half-blind the children? Does it reflect off the wall so that the children cannot properly see what is being shown or written?

When visiting one classroom, because of the angle of the sun I could not read what was written on the board. I asked the children if they could read it and they told me that they could not. Curtains might have solved the problem.

In another classroom in another school, at times the children held their copybooks up to the sides of their faces; the sun was not merely hot but blinding too.

The conditions our children live in at their day-job need to be constantly monitored. It is too easy to assume that all is well when the children do not complain, as they rarely do, not knowing any better. The school authorities, being so busy with huge work loads, much of it bureaucracy, could be unaware of the problems the children are experiencing.

5. Ergonomic Set-Up?

Recently, when visiting an office of a secretary to a CEO, I noticed a splendidly ergonomic desk-computer set-up. The person working there explained that if anyone continues working in an office that is not user-friendly they have only themselves to blame.

Our children spend up to six hours a day sitting at desks. Are the desks and chairs they use ergonomically acceptable? That is, are they well-designed and carefully constructed desks that will help to balance our children's frames and assist them to sit correctly? The following are some questions we might ask regarding the desks and chairs our children use:

+ Are they in good repair?

+ Are they stable?

+ Do the chairs provide support for the child's lumbar region?

+ Are the surfaces of the desks easy to use or are they slippery or too reflective?

+ Are the desks and chairs supplied the right size for my child?

In most schools, except those for the very young, the desks are generally of a similar height and make, even though children vary quite considerably in size. In one first year class at secondary level I have seen children ranging from six-feet-two-inches in height to under five feet. Would it be possible to have seats that are height-adjustable? Imagine a child having to sit all day at a desk that was too high or too low! Maybe they could be issued with adjustable footrests. If the chairs and desks are not adequate, should we be surprised if physical damage is caused?

And if there are double desks supplied where two children sit side by side, what happens if one child is by nature very bulky? Can or should the children complain? I remember travelling through the night for nine hours in a plane. In the seat beside me sat a man of enormous size. The seats were not made for men of his bulk. However, since the plane was full I had to sit in the squashed conditions for the nine-hour journey. A year's journey would be most difficult.

6. Colour Schemes

When we furnish our homes and offices we take great care about colour schemes[1]. Paint, carpet and curtain manufacturers, among others, spend millions of euro or dollars on colour research. According to scientists, colour is important; it can affect moods, attitudes and interactions. Let us consider some of the colours.

It has been ascertained that black is generally depressing and that a black wall or ceiling can give rise to the sensation of being smothered. Dark paint seems to decrease the size and feel of a room. It is also true of course that black might well remind our children of some of their 'heroes' that inhabit their other world.

Blue is considered by many to be relaxing; some colour therapists use it to relieve pain, to lower blood pressure and to promote healing generally. Experts recommend light blue rather than dark blue, especially when used with yellow, for places of study and for offices; dark blue has been found to have a sedative effect.

And what of yellow, orange and red? Yellow is a bright and optimistic colour that seems to help people become organized. Experts regard orange as beneficial in promoting a happy environment and some therapists even say that orange promotes self-esteem and the capacity to forgive. The colour red, on the other hand, has been shown to contribute to the stimulation of energy; it has also been discovered that too much of it makes people irritable and impatient. A red class-room on wet days could spell disaster.

If we choose green or violet we can say that green adds a gentle touch. Green flowers and plants are used to decorate homes, hospitals and businesses. Violet on the other hand is used by psychiatrists to treat their patients. It is considered to have a calming effect on people. Some psychologists say that violet contributes to mental stability. It is often used in prayer rooms.

Therefore, bearing in mind all the above, it is surely irresponsible to paint classrooms without carefully considering the effects of the colours we choose. If, for example, we buy paint for our schools because it was sold at a reduced price, or merely because the colour took someone's fancy, how responsible is that?

In brief, psychiatrists and psychologists tell us that we ignore the effects of colour at our peril.

A further issue regarding colour in schools might be classified as 'the presence of an absence'. Some classes are not painted at all so that the children sit in unpainted concrete containers. It is true that some people can get used to anything, including prisons or even solitary confinement, but such spaces are surely contra-indicated.

In short, the importance of evaluating and monitoring the set-up of the buildings in which our children spend their schooldays cannot be overstressed. The physical size, the noise-levels, the ventilation, the maintenance, the light by which children are expected to learn, temperature levels, the desks, the colours and décor all need to be considered. Parents and teachers need to make sure that our children live lives that reflect their dignity, in other words that they live lives that are happy, colourful and stimulating.

7. Finally - Educational Aids

Finally, we must consider the presence (or absence) of IT and other educational aids in the classroom. For many the use of IT is second nature. Data projectors, power point presentations, carefully edited filmstrips and so on help enormously in the education of our children. In this new millennium it seems at odds with progress that only 'talk and chalk' could still be the norm for a teacher. Lessons can be so enjoyable with music, stimulating activities, problems to consider and discuss, evaluations to be made, ideas to be mulled over. There are recorded views of experts in various disciplines and areas of teaching including the use of symbols and signs and so on, but hands-on activity by the children themselves is regarded as particularly important. Above all other methodologies, the hands-on, carefully organised, acted-upon and reflected-upon activities for children seem to the body of researchers as an unequalled way forward.

The researchers Forsythe, Jolliffe and Stevens[2], for example, say that "even if the teacher tells and shows in an interesting way, they will become bored if they are not involved in the learning...the do method must be applied to all learners, not just a few." Two other researchers, Winch and Gignell[3], conclude that "valid educational experience arises only from self-directed activity". All of them, however, stress that the activity must fit in to what the children already know. If the matter of the subject is merely memorised and regurgitated, there may be no true education.

One remembers the story of the six-year-old child reciting his six-times-tables.

"Six and one are seven, six and two are eight, six and three are nine..." and then an airplane passes overhead.

"Teacher, is that an 737 A300 or a 757... what do you think?"

"Continue please, James"

"Six and four are ten...Teacher, yesterday me and Pete played a game on the computer and I had the best score with twenty-nine, Pete only scored twenty-five."

"What was the game?"

"We were finding cities and major conurbations in Europe. Pete missed two in Italy, one in Spain and one in Germany."

"Major what? .....That's enough tables for today."

Chapter 4: Our Children

What a joy it is to watch our children grow up: their first smiles, their first words, their first steps. And then, practically overnight, they are ready for school. But do we need to evaluate how ready for school they are? Could our child face hidden problems?

1. Eyesight

Parents sometimes take for granted that their child's eyes are perfect. They may not be. Our children should not have to sit in class and be unable to read what is on the board or screen or whatever else is placed in front of them; and our child should also see the teacher clearly. Some do not. Evidently our children should not have to guess at what is happening, no matter how good they are at it. Some do.

Unfortunately, children whose eyes are less than perfect sometimes refuse to wear glasses. On more than one occasion, I found children unable to read what was written on the board, but it took all my persuasive powers to cajole them either to sit nearer the board or purchase glasses. It seems that neither option was 'cool'.

2. Hearing

I have also come across children who were hard of hearing in one ear and indeed others who were quite deaf in both. Their seating positions in the classroom were critical, as was that of the short-sighted child. But often children do not complain; they do not realise that the others see or hear better than they do. As regards hearing, perhaps they do not even realise they have a problem. Parents need to check this carefully.

3. Other Problems

The first child I want to tell you about seemed to be always tired. He often dozed off in class. He was nine, in standard four and seemed to us to be too thin. I suggested to his parents that his heart be checked. It was found that he had a hole in his heart. He was operated on and returned to school, right as rain.

The second case concerns a child in Africa who was stung by a bee. His elder brother assured us that, to the best of his knowledge, his brother was not allergic to bee stings but was asked to inform his parents of the incident and make sure to keep an eye on the young boy. That evening at home the child began to swell up, and being aware of what had happened, the parents whisked him off to hospital where he received the necessary medication. The child was indeed allergic to bee stings.

Another case I want to put before you involved a sixth year student who was doing poorly academically. When he was younger, he was diagnosed as being dyslexic. In the Christmas examinations of his final year, he achieved the equivalent of five Ds at higher level (in those days 5 points). After Christmas, he was recommended to find out if his dyslexia might not in fact be a deficiency called scotopic sensitivity, which may be remedied, and so he went to the Irlen Institute in Dublin[3]. When he returned to school he was wearing coloured glasses. He had no more study problems. In the Leaving Certificate six months later he scored 23 points, an equivalent of five Bs and one C at Higher Level and was able to pursue the career of his choice.

Of course life is not always so simple. People do suffer from problems of sight and hearing and from other physical and mental disabilities and for many there may be no easily available solution. Our children, however, should be given every chance, with every avenue explored should any treatment be necessary. The journey they are on now is their only life.

4. The Habits Our Children Pick Up

We must think too about the habits our children pick up. They probably begin building habits some moments after birth, if not before. Practices to do with dressing, sitting, walking, eating, the taking of exercise, personal hygiene, toilet use, the use of books, responding to aggravating talk, listening to others, being respectful, use of 'bad language' and so on, can become ingrained in them at an early age and difficult to change. We 'oldies' are pleased when children say "Thank you", "Excuse me" or when on buses and trains they give up their seats to elderly passengers.

So, both good and bad habits can be picked up and grow. One child thrilled a group of sixth form parents in his primary school when he played the *'Fantasia Impromptu'* by Chopin; he was only eleven. Over the years he had built up the wonderful habit of avoiding hours of TV viewing and instead practised the piano every day without fail. Another child used to spend time daily in the school chapel before the beginning of lessons and again just before going home; he built up the habit of personal prayer. The authenticity of the child's prayer showed in joyfulness, genuine care for others and transparent authenticity.

On the other hand, I once listened to a group of children and one of them in particular was using rather unacceptable language. When I pointed it out, the child seemed not merely totally unaware of the habit but in fact refused to accept that what I said was true. "F**k it, I never use such language." Then he stopped and almost in disbelief realised what he had just said.

On another occasion, I noticed the smell of tobacco as a student was passing and then observed nicotine stains on his fingers. I asked him if he had begun to smoke. He asked me how I knew. I told him of the nicotine stains and the smell of tobacco. "Do your parents know that you smoke," I asked. "No, they don't" he replied. It seemed they hadn't questioned him. It is sometimes easy to miss the signs. "Why do you not give it up?" I asked. He explained that he had tried three times but had failed; he was only sixteen. It is often so hard for our children to break a habit.

5. Their Own Habits

We must remember then that when our children sit in classrooms they do so with other children, all of whom will have their own habits, some of which will be good and some not so good. What habits will our own children bring to school? What habits will they pick up there?

"Who taught you that?"

"Everybody does it!"

"Why don't you dress properly?"

"Mum, the Principal doesn't mind, so why should you?

"I suppose next you'll tell me you drink and, perish the thought, use drugs"

"Dad, where have you been all these years? Yes, I do drink; but I only take eight to ten pints on weekend nights and yes, I used hash and 'e' but not regularly"

Chapter 5: Children's Gifts

Each child is unique, a 'once off', so it is absurd for our child even to try to become someone else. An education system that demands of children that they become other people is cruel and unjust. It is our own children's unique potential that needs to be actualised, not somebody else's potential.

1. Our Children Drop Hints

What is this potential? From day one our children drop hints as to how they will blossom. I remember a young child not yet able to walk who was already able to undo the screws that held together a gate that cut off the 'escape route' to the upstairs. We have all seen the child who notices the problems of others in a most insightful way or who gets on well with other children; the child who sings almost before beginning to talk; the child with excellent coordination who can kick or hit a ball long distances; the child who can solve mathematical problems; or the child who with ease begins to speak foreign languages. We must listen and observe, we must be there for them and support them as they reveal themselves to us until such time as they become sufficiently strong to battle on their own. Their victory, their joy and ours, is to see them fulfil their God-given, unique potential.

The possession of many fine qualities and talents, however, should not detract from the value of our children striving to become competent in other areas where they may not be particularly talented. A golfer may well be happy with a handicap of 12 – 16 and be quite unperturbed when he meets a twelve-year-old who plays off single figures. A child might achieve two higher-level passes, and the fact that he cannot achieve straight As should not upset him if he has tried his best. However, it can be a waste of both energy and time for children to pursue areas in which they have little talent.

I knew a man once who decided to try his hand at playing a musical instrument. He was an extremely clever man with two academic doctorates to his name. After trying for many years to play the instrument, he finally realised that he could never get beyond a basic level. On the other hand, I have come across young teenagers who, with almost effortless ease, have reached advanced levels in whatever instruments they played. One child may train every day to become a fast runner but, though that child may improve to some degree, unless the talent is there he or she will never achieve any great distinction in running; whereas a gifted child oftentimes will be able to run faster than anybody else without any training at all.

Some children are small and some are tall, some are strong, others are not. Some, as I said, find languages easy, others do not. Some radiate a natural charisma, others do not. There are processes and skills our children can learn, there are methods they can use to achieve results. However, in the  end, children with gifts in a particular field will normally succeed better than others in that same field if they apply themselves. Let us not compare an apple with an orange or a banana with an apple or suggest that one is better than the other or that one should try to become more like the other.

2. The First Gift

The first gift our children possess is the gift of life. We must let them live and not be hustled unnecessarily; in other words, let our children be just that, children. A parent came to me in school to complain about his fourteen-year-old son. He felt his son could be doing much better, could be working much harder. It took some time to explain to the father that, whereas his son probably could work a little harder, putting endless pressure on him was not the way forward; his child was merely a little immature and would blossom if given time and encouragement. His father was not convinced. Like an impatient orchard owner, he wanted summer fruit in spring.

I visited the family in their home and reaffirmed the importance of supporting their son who, after all, was at a difficult age. The father still seemed unconvinced. A short time later there was an accident. As the father was driving his children to school, a lorry sideswiped the father's car, killing the child sitting in the seat behind him, his fourteen-year-old son.

We cannot take the gift of life for granted, nor can we assume that our children will always be in good health or always have the full use of their senses. Some children die young, others are born with disabilities or have to struggle with the results of accidents that have left them permanently crippled or disabled; others suffer from incurable illnesses; other children have debilitating psychological problems. We remember St Martin who once complained that he had no shoes. Then he met a man with no feet. Whether healthy or not, our children are our greatest gift. We must cherish them for as long as they are given to us.

3. Loving People

After life itself, the next most important gift our children have is that they all can be loving people. Some children seem to arrive in the world placid and gentle while others, for whatever reason, begin taking on the world from day one. Those blessed children with loving natures seem to have been given the fast route to happiness. The rest of us have to struggle. But again, whether they are loving and kind or whether they are difficult, all of them have the capacity to become loving people and this quality in our children is more important than all the others. However, of course, we must encourage our children to bring to fruition all of their gifts.

But is it possible for us to discover all of our children's gifts? Probably not! With the help of teachers and advisers, however, we can do our best. If we constantly are there for them, give them priority time and listen carefully to them; if we encourage them, congratulate every effort they make, and recognise their talents and interests, if we notice and acknowledge what 'turns them on' and any successes they achieve, then our children will surely flourish.

On the other hand, it is our failure if we don't give the discovery of our children's gifts our best shot. This failure can take on many different guises. We fail our children when we want them to be something they are not and cannot be. We fail them when we nag them constantly, especially when the school they attend may not be in a position to encourage their unique gifts and expects them to conform to the interests of the majority. However, another way for us to understand reasons for this failure that might make sense to us is to look at former children – ourselves.

4. Given the Opportunity?

Many of us adults are happy in what we do and what was done for us by our parents and schools, but it is also true that some of us were not given the opportunity to accomplish what we reasonably felt we could. Many of us never used or use our special talents. Perhaps we do not know what our talents really are. Did the upbringing and education we received slot us into pigeonholes and make us what we partially have become: ill-fitting clothes?

So, in this state of unknowing, have we gone on working to pay the bills, ignoring the half-heard urgings of our deeper selves? There's the lawyer who really wants to be a musician or painter; the businessman who could have been, and still wants to be, a doctor; the company director who still longs to be a social worker; the civil servant who dreams about being a farmer; the bank official who, possessing all the necessary gifts, really wants to be a teacher; the road maintenance worker, also possessing all the necessary gifts, who will never be a surgeon.

Will this be our children's future? Are we standing quietly aside as our children are being prepared to walk the wide road to quiet frustration, striving to use gifts they do not have or failing to use gifts they have? Will money determine the 'important gifts' or how 'important and successful' our children are?

I remember seeing a large birdcage in which lived a number of beautiful blue and yellow budgerigars. After some years living together the beautiful blues became less blue and the yellows became less yellow and in time there grew up a flock of faded blue-yellow birds.

In brief, in the years to come will our children be living with love, joy and happiness? Will they feel fulfilled, having used their gifts much like a car travelling in top gear on the highway of life? Or will they live in a state of semi-depression and general boredom, filled with an unexplained inner restlessness or a half conscious simmering anger, knowing that they have overlooked waiting-to-be-released gifts. They are much like a car stuck in first gear on the secondary roads away from life's highway or possibly they are on the highway's inside lane, their engine straining and overheating?

One mother who had been very happily busy rearing her seven children and had passed the 'half-ton' had a surprise for her youngest child who was just graduating from secondary school. She informed her child and all the family that she too was going to begin third level to study medicine. Seven years later this wonderful mother and determined woman qualified as a doctor and when last heard of she was happily serving society in her new role. It is possible to change gear.

Chapter 6: Intelligence

Is my child intelligent? This is a question parents often ask themselves. Some parents make their own judgements but sometimes they look for confirmation from others. The feedback they receive may or may not be accurate and balanced.

1. Insightful Educators

Parents who look to the school system for an accurate assessment of their children will seldom have cause to complain; there are some very insightful educators. On occasion, however, the feedback could be misleading and/or unhelpful.

'A fine child but …is struggling… is below average'

'Yes, your child is a fine person but no, not an academic'

'A weak student'

'A very average student'

'Seems little interested in school'

'Tends to be distracted'

'Is disruptive'

The above assessments, when predicated of our child, may well be true but they do not tell the story of either the child's potential or the child's uniqueness.

There was once a student who did badly at school and was regularly punished for poor work and lack of effort. The student failed some of the courses numerous times and only on his third attempt qualified for a third level college and then only near the bottom of the student intake of 102. In time, this poor student became an author, soldier, journalist, politician and Nobel prize-winner in literature. He also was one of the most important leaders in British and world history; his name was Winston Leonard Spencer Churchill KG, OM, CH, PC, FRS, best known as Prime Minister of the United Kingdom during World War II.

What then of my child?

2. There Are Thousands

Winston Churchill is only one case; there are tens of thousands. Let us suppose a child does very well in school and the parents realise she has no problem there. Does this necessarily mean that the child is very intelligent? Not always. It merely means that the child is academically bright and possesses a high IQ.

What is IQ? IQ, or intelligence quotient, generally refers to two and sometimes three kinds of ability: linguistic ability, logical-mathematical ability and sometimes spatial intelligence. The first two areas, and sometimes the third, are targeted by nearly all school systems. So, if a child performs well in these areas, the child will normally be successful in school, assuming reasonable application.

3. 'Intelligences'

However there are at least five other intelligence areas or 'intelligences' according to today's research, particularly that of a Professor Gardner of Harvard. From his research, he points out that some children though not particularly gifted in the three IQ areas, may be gifted in other areas and, in real terms, be highly intelligent. The corollary is also true: those who are very competent in the first three areas of IQ may not be so much so in these other areas.

Some schools do try to target these other non-IQ intelligence areas or abilities and are often successful, but unfortunately government examination systems in general only rate the first three. So the temptation for many schools, particularly 'cram schools', is largely to sacrifice the 'non-IQ abilities' for 'good results' in public examinations; so much so that some schools only take in high IQ students, regardless of their other gifts and abilities. Needless to say, publishing school league tables further entrenches these misunderstandings. What are these other abilities?

Rather than assume the meaning of any of the eight-and-a-half 'intelligences' noted by Professor Gardner[5], I shall briefly outline each one.

The three 'intelligences' targeted by nearly all examination systems:

1. Linguistic intelligence will reveal itself when our child shows sensitivity to spoken and written language. Without too much difficulty, our child will display an ability to learn languages, and be able to use language. Our child will not merely remember information through language but will have the gift of expression in poetry and rhetoric.

2. Logical-mathematical intelligence will reveal itself when our child shows the capacity to analyse problems, and logically deduce answers. Mathematics and scientific investigation will not pose a problem for such a child.

3. Spatial intelligence reveals itself when our children show the potential to recognize and use the patterns of space. This includes perceiving the visual world accurately, being able to transform and modify things working with their per-

ceptions and then the ability to recreate aspects of their visual experience even if the experienced object is now absent.

The 'intelligence' areas that may not be directly addressed in schools and lack of which may not adversely affect gaining excellent academic examination results are described as follows:

4. Musical intelligence will be revealed when our child can perform with skill and can compose and appreciate the patterns of musical composition and pitch; when tones and rhythms are easily grasped.

5. Bodily-kinaesthetic intelligence shows itself when our children can coordinate mental and physical activity. This reveals itself in the capability to involve themselves in coordinated activity in everyday pursuits. This is not only obvious in a facility to play games but also in working with their hands, working with machines, and using their bodies to communicate without words. It also includes their mode of walking and carrying themselves. There is, in all this co-ordination, a sense of timing. Basically, the children, by using their whole body or parts of the body, are in fact solving the problems of daily living.

6. Interpersonal intelligence reveals itself when our children show the capacity to understand the intentions, motivations and desires of other people. Through this understanding, the child in time will normally be effective in working with others.

7. Intrapersonal intelligence reveals itself when our children show the capacity to understand themselves, appreciate what their own feelings and fears are and what really motivates them.

8. Naturalist intelligence enables our child to recognize, categorize and draw upon certain features of the environment.

8.5 Spiritual intelligence, in the view of Howard Gardner, is only partially provable. He feels that there are problems around the 'content' of spiritual intelligence. It is hard, in his view, to 'nail it down', to evaluate it. For him, it would be necessary to define it partly through its effect on other people. We will deal with this later.

In brief, without musical, bodily-kinaesthetic, interpersonal, intrapersonal, naturalistic, spiritual and indeed spatial intelligences it is possible in our educational systems to be 'extremely successful', gain top grades and enter university to pursue the most stringent courses. This applies in almost all countries. This simplistic attitude seems sad in face of the complexity of our human species and the growing body of research that questions the validity of such an educational paradigm.

4. The Complexity of the Gifts

It is, therefore, important to realise and accept the complexity of us humans and that the gifts of linguistic and logical-mathematical and spatial abilities do not cover the vast number of gifts our children possess. Our children are much more than their achievements in these areas. Unfortunately, despite protestations to the contrary, it is like the seed that fell on the pathway and was gobbled up by the birds; our acceptance of this truth is often merely notional and not real, and often applies to schools.

In real terms, if we look at the daily routine of many of our children's school days, month after month, year after year, they are full of lessons that generally confine themselves to fostering linguistic and logical-mathematical abilities, while the many other areas of our child's intelligence are sometimes given scant attention. Yes, there are sometimes sports and practical subjects offered for those who are willing or are chosen; and in a few cases there is training in music and musical instruments, though this can be too rare and generally must be pursued elsewhere.

Schools often feel that if the children do well academically or in the IQ areas, they, the schools, have done their job, and the children whose gifts lie elsewhere and who do not fare particularly well in the examinations can be considered 'average', 'weak' or 'a failure'. Look at the American SAT tests, the British A levels, the Irish Leaving Certificate, the European International Baccalaureate, they all stress linguistic, logical-mathematical and spatial intelligences. What happens to the child with a low IQ?

"My daughter did very well"

"Yes, but she is very intelligent"

"My son got his first choice in university"

"He is intelligent too"

"Mine didn't... after the fourteen years of schooling"

"Neither did mine... My son can't speak any foreign language well. He is weak at mathematics, knows something about geography and business subjects but after that there's not too much. He can play the guitar a little...thirteen years... it isn't much return... all the same he is happy"

5. Success at School

Does success at school mean the child will do well later on in life? No, I am afraid it doesn't. Many who do well at school do have happy and fruitful lives. However I have seen children who at school seemed to possess good academic ability and did well here and later in University examinations, but once outside the system they did not fare too well. (There is a rumour of a young man who on his wedding night ecstatically declared to his wife "E= MC²"...)

So does failure in school mean my child does not have a high IQ? It is close to impossible to say. If a child cannot cope with school or finds it too difficult, is not a late developer and is not suffering from a psychological trauma or physical disability – such as bad eyesight, chemical imbalance, side effects of necessary medication or sundry other reasons – then the child may not be academically intelligent and may not have a high intelligence quotient.

So if my child does not have a high IQ, what then?

I used the words 'may not have a high IQ' and 'is not a late developer, is not suffering from a psychological trauma or physical disability– such as bad eyesight, chemical imbalance, side effects of necessary medication or sundry other reasons'. It is important to realise that life is most complex. I have in my years in schools come across numerous children with high IQs who for one or more of the above reasons did not fare well in school. I would particularly like to highlight the problem of immaturity or the late developer. Some children by nature are late developers, but the systems push them along year by year though they are not ready for it. Such late developers are expected to fit into the school system, rather than the school system fitting itself to them so that they can prosper. A general regime with yearly examinations and final examinations at a given age for all, regardless of maturity, is unfortunately more or less the norm. I have known children who did not fare well academically in school who later became outstanding academics and who spent their lives happily as such. But there is more.

6. The Last Ten to Fifteen Years

It is only in the past ten to fifteen years that nearly all of our detailed knowledge about the brain has been discovered. For all these years we have been calling our small lake an ocean. Happily we now stand closer to the ocean's shoreline and realize that we know very, very little about humankind. Our small-lake view espoused by most school systems generally only recognized IQ, or intelligence quotient, and suggested to us that only those with a high IQ were the intelligent ones. When our children were found wanting in this area they, and we, often felt or were told that they were not intelligent.

Have we not over the years heard parents talking about their children: "Poor child", "And what are we going to do? The youngster works so hard at school but is very weak". Modern findings have a much more thorough and benign good-news story to tell us, even if we still know very little so far.

It is becoming more and more clear, through research, that besides IQ there is also EQ, the latter representing emotional intelligence or the capability to be intelligent in the field of emotions. Professor Gardner, as we saw earlier, speaks about interpersonal and intrapersonal intelligences. And this competence in empathy and self-awareness, it transpires, often matters much more in the running of our world than IQ. So what is this EQ?

Chapter 7: Emotional & Spiritual Intelligences

Over many years the on-going research of top American researchers, Coleman[6], McClelland, the Hay Group, Boyatzis and many others, has revealed that between 80-90% of the major CEOs in the USA do not hold their positions because of their IQ capability but rather because of their high EQ or emotional intelligence. Today's leaders, they discovered, generally work with their emotional intelligence, which is centred in a different part of the brain to IQ.

EQ is the name given to emotional intelligence. Emotional Intelligence includes the ability, through interpersonal and intrapersonal gifts, to inspire collective emotions in a positive direction. Children with EQ can clear away the negative impact of ever-present toxic emotions. This ability not merely facilitates work to proceed in our world but it actually helps people give of their best and achieve far more than could have been hoped for initially. This leadership achievement is caused by what is called "the resonance effect". This effect is so called because when people feel mentally in tune with the leader they resonate, are happily involved and achieve more. Neither is there need for much verbal input from the leader; often, little needs to be said. There is, in business jargon, "more signal, less noise".

In the various schools in which I have been involved over the years it was often apparent that some of the children were gifted with a high EQ. One had only to watch the playground to see the child with the high EQ. These children were organisers, they got people involved who otherwise were not interested and they achieved results and won competitions merely by their being there as a source of strength to the whole group.

I remember a football match where a child with notable EQ was hurt and on the bench. His team was faring badly. However, in the second half the child joined his team. It was as if a different team was playing. The team became alive, full of hope and eventually won the game. How did the child do it? EQ. It can be argued that the provision of sports and other activities that require leadership does in fact promote EQ in schools. But a scientific and more proactive approach to the development of these gifts in our children would seem to be needed.

2. Will Be Positive

So, if a child possesses a high EQ, his or her presence will be positive, supportive and many aspects of our school and home lives will improve. Such improved situations will show on faces, in voices and gestures; feelings will become upbeat. This 'feeling good' lubricates mental efficiency. A parent or teacher with a high IQ is of course well capable of managing a home or school; but if also equipped with emotional intelligence he or she can lead and, with the 'resonance effect', create positive attitudes and greater personal growth all round. It was Einstein who reportedly said: "We should take care not to make the intellect our god. It has of course powerful muscles but no personality. It cannot lead, it can only serve".

I remember a student who, while learning how to use his relational skills, spent two weeks with an autistic child. The autistic child did not speak, nor had ever spoken. Nevertheless, each day the student sat with this child and spoke to him about all sorts of things. After nine days, the second last day of his two-week stint, the student announced to the child that he was on his second last day. A tear appeared on the autistic child's face and he spoke for the first time ever. "Don't go, Robbie," he said.

It is my view, then, that we could seriously consider teaching our children to think not only with their heads but also with their bodies and their emotions, with their spirits and their visions, their hopes, their sense of meaning and their sense of value. In other words, we can help our children understand and perfect their EQ capability through practice, with an awareness of its scope. In due course, many of our children will not just manage situations but will learn to lead with resonance, inspiring collective emotions in a positive direction, clearing away the negative impact of toxic emotions, helping people to give of their best and achieve far more than could have been hoped for initially.

3. SQ

Professor Gardner has problems with the idea of a spiritual intelligence. He maintains that we cannot know for certain that it exists. As earlier stated, his difficulty centres on the 'content' of spiritual intelligence. Others, however, have no doubts whatsoever. Researchers call this important third intelligence capability SQ[7]. It is proposed that this SQ, or Spiritual Intelligence, is distinct from both IQ and EQ and is found in a different area of the brain. Many of our children are gifted with a high SQ. What is SQ?

As our IQ helps us to think logically and rationally, as EQ enables us to manage those parts of our lives that we call interpersonal and intrapersonal, so SQ helps us to think creatively in an insightful way that can be both rule-making and rule-breaking. SQ is the ability of people to deal with questions such as: "why?" and "what if?" It is not, as the name might suggest a religious-belief mechanism. Neither is this SQ value-dependent or indeed culture-dependent; humans use it as they strive to uncover the ultimate meaning of life. Most importantly, it guides both our children and us in our search for truth.

There is also a story about the captain of a plane flying over the South Pacific. He radios to the nearest control tower stating that he and his crew are breaking the world record, surpassing the previous highest speed for their type of plane. The control tower congratulates them but then asks: "Where are you going?" There is a pause and the captain replies: "I don't know...!" SQ was needed.

4. Outward v Inward

Unfortunately, oftentimes in our homes and in our schools children are trained to look outward rather than inward, to focus on facts and practical problems in the external world, to be achievement-oriented. Rarely enough is it strongly suggested in our exam-oriented schooling that youth should seriously and constantly reflect on themselves and their inner lives, emotions and motivation. They are not often encouraged or given the space to reflect on what they believe in or on what they really value and why.

Their working days are filled mostly with activity and their potentially silent times are often filled with noise. We parents and teachers need to make time and space for reflection and silence both for them and for ourselves.

The outcome of support and encouragement to do this will be that our children will begin to show a growing capacity for flexibility of thought; they will be inspired by a broader vision of the possibilities for an enhanced way of living, a way of life inspired by core human values; they will make connections and see commonalities in diverse things. They will bring to the surface the assumptions that they and we live by – assumptions of which we all need to be aware. They will become more reflective and responsible, more authentic and willing to act in ways that require courage and self-belief.

If today we listen to the questioning of our SQ children, they are asking how they can cope in our society. They are pointing out that they are not particularly interested in merely continuing willy-nilly what we, the older generations, have hatched for them. They point to our economics-based wars, pandemic poverty and hunger, the lack of clear rules and values and little sign of personal responsibility. "Are authentic relationships and real caring not primary for humanity to live and survive... have you missed the larger picture?" they ask us. Yes, there is a great need in our society for children who are gifted with a high SQ. Who else will consider and point out our many over-looked problems?

5. Questions?

One boy in class raised his hand and asked the following question: "You were talking of quality of products and services and a commitment to never-ending economic growth. What I would like to know is – what are we growing towards and where will it all lead us in the end?"

One teacher explained: "Those teenagers who think deeply know that to interact properly in our technological, goal-driven world, they need to deal efficiently with textbooks, timetables and goal-oriented planning, but at the same time the more thoughtful ones realise the necessity to integrate it all into the wider context of a truly meaningful, authentic and purpose-filled life. If we look at the more insightful middle-twenties adults today they are beginning to walk their paths, to live their dreams, their relationships, and their work and to strive for their goals.

One such young person explained to me: "To be successful as humans we must be deeply committed and dedicated. But we must also work from the centre of our beings. If we act from the expectations of society or others it could be catastrophic."

Another added: "Each of us must try to make our own personal input and not somebody else's. I initially tried to be an architect but I found out that I didn't have the required gifts. Now I am very happy working with the gifts I do have. The youth of today, if they listen to their deep thinkers, won't go far wrong."

Chapter 8: Choosing a School

We have considered school and our children's gifts, we now ask the question: "Which school should my child attend?" Let us, therefore, take the case of a husband and wife who have four children and consider some of the problems these parents face when choosing schools for their children.

"We have four children ranging from 10 to 14 years of age. We are considering moving house and we must ask ourselves "What kind of education will our children receive near our new home?"

1. Janette

Firstly there is Janette, our eldest child. Janette is generally a happy child. She is good at mathematics and has a reasonable flair for languages and loves reading; she is also a good worker. Janette, in our view, is a balanced child and gives us no hassle. However, what might come against her in a new school is that she is not a particularly 'social animal' since, although she has good friends, she does not make friends too easily. Further, she is not 'into games', not being particularly athletic or interested. Not to be involved in games is oftentimes seen as a drawback in second level schools. Nevertheless, on balance, we feel that she should fit in well to the scheme of things with her capability in languages and mathematics, which are obviously the capabilities most rewarded in schooling today.

2. Michael

Michael, the second child, is a different kettle of fish. He, unlike Janette, has difficulty in grasping mathematics and although he appreciates language, he is not particularly interested in reading or indeed in anything that keeps him away from his friends and his games. Michael loves sports of all types, particularly football, and is reasonably good at most of them. Give him a ball and he is quite happy playing all day with his friends. He has countless friends and seems to get on very well with everybody. Neither is his friendship confined to his own age group; he is capable of beguiling almost everybody he meets. The shopkeeper, the bus driver, the postman, the policeman, the people on our street all greet him and are greeted by him. At home he charms us all so that it is almost impossible to get him to go to bed if a TV programme he is watching is unfinished. "OK, but only this time." But it hasn't all been easy for him; he has been quite ill a number of times but somehow coped remarkably each time with both the illness and his incapacity.

It is our contention that he is an intelligent person. Michael's intelligence, however, is in the areas of interpersonal and intrapersonal relationships and in facing personal rather than academic difficulties and problems. But will Michael get on well in the local school? Will the education provided consider and enhance his specific gifts? Will the school, while offering many programmes, have an ethos that rewards all gifts or only academic achievement? In brief, will the system properly recognise his non-academic gifts? If not, will his friendships sustain him and will he be able to support the long hours of academic pursuit in which he is not interested? He could end up with a happy group of 'non-achievers'.

3. Gabriel

Gabriel, the third child, might be classed as a definite non-academic. He, at the moment, has little interest in any of the normal main-line subjects of school. Mind you, he isn't entirely hopeless at mathematics and languages but he gets bored fairly easily. On the positive side he is very good with his hands. He can make things with incredible precision. He has already made a desk, chairs and various oddments for the house. Also, he can cook and often does. We bought him a tool kit for his birthday and now he fixes any breakages in the house. I suppose he could be said to show good kinaesthetic intelligence.

He is good at sport where, like his work with his hands, his coordination, timing, delicacy and precision of movement are very advanced for his age. Will he fit into the school system? Along with the main subjects, do the local schools offer practical subjects: woodwork, building construction, social and scientific, metalwork and a well-organised PE and games programme? If so, yes, he should survive. If not, what will happen to his gifts? Will they have to be left aside, to become mere holiday pursuits?

4. Elizabeth

Our youngest child, Elizabeth, seems to be a very bright and highly sensitive young lady and already, at the age of 10, considers the most problematic issues, far beyond her years. In school it seems that she finishes the class work in less than half the normal time and keeping her busy is often a problem for her teachers. Besides finding no difficulty with the various subjects offered, she is also good at music and gives us great joy when she decides to play for us.

Interestingly, she is also quite a spiritual person and furthermore seems at home in religious activities. She is also most interested in nature, she 'knows' and can name every animal, bird, insect, tree and flower in the neighbourhood. There is a swing in the garden and she often spends time just thinking and watching. But at home she is only occasionally interested in normal study and doing homework; she seems to be more interested in 'more fundamental issues' to quote her teacher in the last school.

She has already read many of the books at home and many from the local library – she even seems to understand some of the books in foreign languages without much effort. Our problem now is whether this shy child of ours will find a place and be happy in the schools in the area. Will they challenge her sufficiently? Will they have a good language department and a good music programme? And will they have good religious education programmes that will help explain to her the true meaning of spirituality; will the teachers be able to leave room for the questioner?

Our hope is that all the gifts of our children will be helped to grow in the school system but we might have reason to worry that this may not happen. Basically, as these children of ours sit in their separate classes, will their specific gifts be recognised or will they be asked to follow the 'normal and average' of the class. And when we read their school reports, will we find them summarised as 'intelligent', 'average' or 'fairly weak'? Or will the words 'disruptive', 'distracted' and 'not working' be used to describe them?

In other words, will the schools' understanding of intelligence be largely based on being a good academic so that if our children do not show linguistic intelligence or logical-mathematical intelligence they will be relegated to the also-rans? Or could we hope for a more enlightened system that considers all types of intelligence and educates our children accordingly? And will the system allow our children to mix with all those other children who show different and varied capabilities? We are acutely aware that their life at school is not a preparation for life, it is their life and it may be their only life. Our first-born child, who would now be seventeen, died at the age of ten."

5. Children's Teachers

Since our children with their multiple intelligences go to school for over thirty-three weeks a year, they look to their teachers to help them fulfil their potential. But what kind of teachers will they have? Will the teachers have good IQs who clearly understand what is to be taught and how it is to be taught? Will the teachers possess good EQs and understand the children, resonate with them and lead them rather than manage them?

Will the teachers have high SQs and appreciate that beyond the syllabi, which largely deal with linguistic, spatial and mathematical-logical intelligences, there are other intelligences? Will each child with his or her unique gifts and personality blossom under the guidance of their various teachers?

Will each teacher who teaches our children be interested in being a teacher? Will the children feel cherished by their teacher? Will the teachers pass on a love for their subjects to the children; or will some of the children's teachers be teaching subjects in which they have no interest and do not adequately understand, due to the problems of timetabling or other reasons?

Will some teachers find themselves merely 'putting in the hours', slavishly following textbooks, being too tired or disinterested to do anything more? Will insistence on the rules of the school and the demand for attention and conformity allow for our children's questions during their lessons?

We always hope that our children end up after each school year with a growing love and understanding of the subjects they have been taught and a deeper knowledge of who they are and their place in the order of things. But will this hope normally become a reality? Can parents, within reason, make sure that this will happen? Can parents be assured that their children will blossom and will not just sit there most of the year with a few uninterested or inadequate teachers, ending up the year with little knowledge and little interest, both in the subject areas these teachers covered and possibly, therefore, in their own personal areas of giftedness? In these latter cases self-esteem and growth of a child's personality can be stunted. No school is perfect but we have a responsibility to our children who are gifted to us for a short time, to make sure that their personalities and gifts are given every chance to blossom.

6. A Choice?

To care for children is a truly awesome responsibility; they are the future of our societies, the future of the human race. In this regard, then, we must ask whether parents should have any say in the choice of their children's teachers. Should they have any input if they believe that the teachers of their children are either excellent or prove to be ineffectual?

The question of whether in justice children should be allowed to stay in classes where little education is taking place must also be faced. These are thorny questions and most difficult to address but they should be addressed. Again, in this regard, should parents leave all the assessment of teachers to the schools or have they a right to become seriously involved in finding out how good their children's educators are – though we know that education is much more than results in examinations? Will teachers, school administrators and governments allow this involvement? Should they? In short, if the best is to be achieved for our children, should parents be expected merely to accept unquestioningly the 'status quo' regarding teachers in the schools their children attend?

In one school in which I was involved, letters came from the parents in considerable numbers regarding one teacher. The teacher was so good that all the children wanted to be in the class taught by that teacher. Evidently it was not possible, but it did underline that all children like flowers in spring, have an unquenchable, built-in thirst for full blossoming. In the pop music world we all realise that some groups 'make it' while others do not, no matter how hard they try; might it be the same with teachers? Would the Teachers' Unions concur?

7. How Much?

There is no perfect situation in our world but how much could our children reasonably learn during their twelve or thirteen years of primary and secondary schooling? How great is the gap between what they could learn and what they actually learn? How much of a gap is there between the people they actually become and the people they could have become? Would this gap lessen if administrators, teachers and parents spent more time together in dialogue, reflection, study and serious evaluation? Is there adequate on-going evaluation and testing of all the personal skills and abilities of our children and not merely of the narrow IQ skills? Likewise, is there adequate evaluation and testing of the IQ skills and of all the personal skills and abilities of teachers before they enter the school work force? What will future generations think of us, the parents and teachers of this generation?

Chapter 9: 'Something Else?'

But maybe, after all, there is a larger problem. Is it possible that there are more pervasive and formative forces influencing our children than either the family or the school, forces few of us adequately consider and about which we therefore know little?

Warren[9], a well-known researcher in education, suggests that it might be the curricula of the marketers, 'teen' music, political messages, media and violence that most affect our children today. Let us consider this.

1. The Marketers

We know that marketers who sell music, clothes, cars, washing-up liquid, newspapers, bank loans, drugs – whatever – expend vast monies on research to make more and more profits. We also know that their research aims to make sure that as many of us as possible will want what they are selling. I remember going for a walk and passing a group of actors with a film crew who were on their thirtieth take. The take was of an actor removing a box of a particular brand of cigarette out of his pocket and passing on a cigarette from the box to another actor while five or six others looked on. The whole action took around five to six seconds. When I returned from my walk the group were on their ninety-third take.

The marketers normally do whatever it takes to sell a commodity and many are eminently successful. As we know, all over the world 'top' brands are both available and bought in very large quantities. What do our children ask for or, if we let them, demand? Having lived in the 'Developing World' for many years, I felt extremely powerless and sad as I watched well-known brand names being worn by children, some of whom did not have enough to eat. One day I saw a child in a shanty town with a well-known brand name stretched over his distended belly.

2. Teen Music

Cole[10] and others who have done detailed research on the effects of music, suggest that music can inspire individuals, create bonding, predispose people to live spiritual lives and generally promote greater creativity. Unfortunately, as Cole points out, it also can cause our children to become discouraged, corrupt their personalities and disrupt the society in which they, and we, live. He talks of 'codability' and the significant emotional power of music that can "enhance feelings of lust, religious sentiment, patriotic fervour or urges towards rebellion". Could this be so? It is worth considering.

Many people think that children do not know the lyrics of songs. Having carried out a quantitative survey with school children, it became clear to me that the vast majority of them do, in fact, know very accurately the words of a huge repertoire of songs. Indeed, if we watch the vast crowds at pop concerts we will see nearly all of the tens of thousands singing along with the performers, line after line, verse after verse. Evidently, if children listen to songs and sing and hum them to themselves over and over again, day after day and week after week, they will remember them.

So should parents and teachers investigate what songs our children are listening to; what lyrics and messages they are 'hearing and feeling'? Should we be interested in this whole 'other world' whose values they are being taught to sing and express every day? It is my firm view that we should. I feel that we do need to study the words and emotional content of our children's music, and the accompanying videos of each song. What particularly struck me recently, when talking to a group of young teenagers, was that MTV was very high on their list of 'the most watched channels'. This fact, added to the daily parade of walkmans, disc players and iPods being carried everywhere by so many, suggests that music could significantly influence our children's lives.

I remember the story of an eight-year-old child who was sitting on a sofa in his home watching TV. He was on his own for some time when suddenly his grandmother walked into the room. Immediately the child changed the channel on the TV. "Why did you change the channel?" The grandmother asked. "Gran," the child replied, "I don't think the channel was suitable for you."

3. 'World' of Spin

I recently read a letter sent some time ago to an American mother[11]. It was from her son who was behind the lines in the first Iraq war. It concerned 'the enemy'.

> "Mom, some of them (the Iraqi soldiers) were deaf or blinded, they didn't have helmets. Hell, they didn't even have shoes. When I approached them, I'd have to keep talking, talking as gently as I could. Trying to communicate with my tone of voice that I would not hurt them...I offered them food, and they bit through the plastic wrappings."

Political 'sound bites' – often less than a few paragraphs in a newspaper or a few minutes on radio or TV – 'inform' our children and us of what is happening in the world. What is worse, we seem to accept that generally we are being told the truth. However if we investigate more deeply, it now seems sure that politicians, even if they know the truth, too often seem to tell us only what they want us to believe. And since our governments and leaders are well aware that obsession with money and 'success', sex and sport, love and romance are the predominant interests for the vast majority of us humankind, we are left in the dark, believing that all is as we have been told it is. Should we have this kind of faith in our politicians and the media?

We could consider what has happened in the world in the past few decades:

- The 'taking out' of Saddam Hussein while collaterally killing or maiming hundreds of thousands of ordinary people, now estimated to be close to one million. Why? Why not Zimbabwe, Sudan or the Democratic Republic of the Congo where untold atrocities are occurring?

- Continued support by the rich world of numerous malevolent regimes. Think of the human rights record of some of the Middle East countries, not to mention Guantanamo.

- The continued raping of third world economies where the rich countries tell the poor countries: a) how much they, the poor countries, are to pay for the rich world's commodities and services and b) how much they, the poor countries, will be paid by the rich countries for the poor countries' commodities and services.

- Exorbitant interest on the loans given by the rich countries to the poor countries. The Philippines is a good example. In 1990 the Philippines owed the rich world 25 billion dollars. The Philippine government as a result cut spending on education, health and so on. By 1995 the Philippine government had paid back 21 billion to the rich world. However, because of the exorbitant interest rates their debt, despite the 21 billion payback, had risen to 28 billion.

- Millions of children dying of hunger – around one every seven seconds – despite food being available in the world and First World farmers being paid to keep their land fallow.

As stated above, our governments and leaders are well aware that obsessions with money and 'success', sex and sport, love and romance are the predominant interests for the vast majority of us, which may explain why we have done so little to make sense of these obsessions. What do our children think of all this? And what will happen now that the money markets are under threat; will we now sit up and take notice of what is happening in our world?

4. 'The Media'

There are many members of the media who work very hard in television, radio, newspapers and magazines. These people forage and bring to light much that has a significant bearing on our lives. Without them important information could easily be covered up or ignored. As we experienced in the second Iraq war and in Afghanistan, through their use of modern technology, we were shown many events as they happened – though it is true that few countries were given the whole truth. If we compared, for example, the news on British, French and American television networks, the whole truth was still a casualty of war. Nevertheless, we were given a more factual insight than heretofore into the unfolding events.

However, there are other members of the media who influence television, radio, newspapers and magazines for whom truth seems unimportant. These people report what sells, what makes their shareholders a profit, provided serious litigation is avoided. We and our children are showered with innuendos and half-truths on multiple topics.

Let us, for example, examine their use of photographs and video cuts. I have seen numerous photographs; some flattered and some misled some were damaging to the viewer. I have seen others with utterly misleading captions or had headings that applied to other columns and had nothing to do with the person, persons or events in the photograph. I have also seen numerous videos that, through a speed change, transformed normal people into menacing or silly ne'er-do-wells. The tricks that are used to mislead are legion. Unfair videos and photographs have damaged thousands, can promote many agendas – and do.

Sleight-of-hand statistics is another strategy. Statistics reveal much at the surface level but can hide essentials and be manipulated to serve whatever impression or agenda is desired. I remember going to Brussels to find the OECD up-to-date statistics on education. Having found them, I returned home. A short time later when certain reports were published, the statistics were significantly misleading and agenda-driven.

And headlines can sell newspapers. The greater the sales, the more valuable the advertisement spaces become. Unfortunately, if the facts of any given headline are shown to be inaccurate or misleading, any rare apology proffered can be just as damaging as the headline. Furthermore, apologies are normally hidden in some out of the way place.

5. Violence

Bearing in mind the above, it is important to mention the often hidden, often taken-for-granted, tired acceptance of violence. Violence can be found at the heart of our societies. It is especially prevalent in DVDs/videos, television, films, music, words of songs and video games. Most cultures today are already quite violent; but in recent times there are signs that violence is significantly on the increase. In our educational provision we, parents and teachers, need to be aware of what is happening and what has happened and what this generation is facing. Today some say that we might even question whether the message of violence is deeper and has more influence on our children than any messages of peace, forgiveness and caring.

In a very short time, violence and its acceptance has become a living, frightening reality, knocking at our front door, staring at us from the screens in our sitting rooms and sneaking through our computer terminals. We could ask whether it is still possible to make our homes and our schools places of peace, joy and safety. But what can we do? Possibly we could make sure that political representatives are put in place that will really address the situation. All over the world various initiatives are being taken and many of them are proving quite successful. But we must want serious initiatives to be taken before it is too late.

For many years I lived abroad and when I came home to Ireland it was delightful to be able to walk around the streets, by-ways and forest walks without fear. Anyone I met was usually friendly, never hostile. The police were a benign, generally liked, respected and unarmed force. In those days, the 'seventies, the Law Courts almost came to a standstill when there was a murder, so infrequently did they occur. And today? A benign police force still exists but many of them are armed. Murders occur every few days and walking the streets, by-ways and forest walks can be dangerous. Must it be so? Will it get worse? Are we ignoring what is happening or just hoping it will go away?

6. The Frog

As I look at the situation I am often reminded of the story of the frog that was asked by the chef in a hotel to jump into a pot of boiling water. Having put its foot into the pot, the frog immediately removed it and said, "Under no circumstance will I jump into that pot... you must think I am stupid." "Fair enough," said

the chef, "I won't ask you to do that but do have a swim in this other pot of nice warm water." The frog put its toe into the warm water and smiled and then jumped in. It swam and enjoyed itself. "This is great, thank you, Chef," said the frog. The chef in the meantime turned up the gas slightly under the pot so that in a short time the frog got warmer and warmer and cozier and cozier and just a little sleepy. "This is wonderfully relaxing," said the frog. In a short time it fell asleep and soon became boiled frog. The temperature in our society is rising.

Chapter 10: Back Home

Their day-job over, and the children once again pack up their bags and prepare to go home. Whether they had a happy day or not, whether there were good conditions for education in the school or not, whether their good habits were reinforced or not, they now leave the school buildings.

1. The Way Home

On the way home, whether directly or not, our children once again turn on their mobile phones, their Walkmans, Disc Players and iPods. From now until bedtime their education will continue at full pace. The people they now talk to, the music messages they hear, the hidden, unspoken, verbalized or non-verbalized messages on their phones, videos, DVDs, television programmes, in books, newspapers and magazines, will change their perspectives and their knowledge base and their inner lives.

2. To Whom Are They Talking

But to whom are they talking and what do these people know, understand, believe, hope or live for? If we saw our children talking to an unknown person at length outside the supermarket we would become quickly involved but today our children can do just that on their phones or computers without our knowledge. Indeed, some parents rightly worry about their children coming home late from school or from a disco or party and they then feel secure and relieved when they arrive in the front door. What is sometimes forgotten is that waiting for them on their computers in chat rooms or elsewhere on the internet are forces and experiences that could be much more damaging than anything experienced on their way home or on their night out.

Also, as our children watch the 'soaps' and other seemingly innocuous programmes, they are in a way watching a 'different programme' to us adults. The meaning of the symbols, gestures and words often relate to their 'other world'.

So, when our children say 'goodnight' what kind of an educational day have they experienced? And what will tomorrow be like? And what will they be like the day after tomorrow?

3. What Have They Learned In School?

As suggested throughout this short book, it is quite impossible to find out what precisely our children learned during their time at school. We have yet to fathom the depths of the unconscious, the real motivations that move them to act, the symbols that affect them deeply, the intellectual, emotional and spiritual worlds that they have within them. However, we can assess to some extent what the children know and what skills they have and what they generally seem to believe in and hope for.

So we ask the question: after all the hard work, the years of classes, the homework, the school tests and examinations, the public examinations, the penances, the suspensions, the letters to and from the school, the parents' meetings, the tears and the sleepless nights, what have our children actually provably learned?

Rather than giving statistics that can be used to push many agendas, let us ask the questions that we all will be able to answer through our day-to-day experiences. We are talking now about the normal eighteen-year-old who leaves school after twelve or thirteen years of primary and secondary education.

• Mother Tongue

Can our children grammatically and coherently write in their mother tongue and can they spell accurately? Do they have a love of literature and poetry in their mother tongue? Are they well read? Can they write letters and speeches and speak well in public? Do they have an extensive vocabulary?

• Foreign Languages

Can they speak a foreign language fluently, preferably more than one, after the years of study? Can they read and understand the spoken word, enjoy a film or play in that language (or languages)? Do they enjoy reading its literature and poetry? In all this it is important to evaluate what was actually learned in school as distinct from what was learned as a result of other influences such as visiting a foreign country in order to learn the language or doing extra courses outside the school.

• Numeric Literacy

Are our children numerically literate so that they can read and understand the numbers used in everyday life? Do they understand banking, loans, percentages and mortgages? Do they understand the incidence of taxation in budgets? Can they work out the meaning of numbers on labels, on medicines, on food products and other products: milligrams, centilitres and so on? Do they understand statistics and how they are produced and used? Are they *au fait* with the broad basics of economics?

+ Generally

There are many other subjects but, in brief, if our sons and daughters are walking through the countryside, can they name the flora and fauna, the insect and bird life? If the car breaks down can they normally fix it? Can they cook tasty meals for practicality and for delight in living? If there is a problem in the house/apartment related to painting, wallpaper, electricity, dampness, plumbing, shelving and so on, can they deal with it adequately? If a child gets sick, can our young adults diagnose the normal illnesses and deal with them safely? Can they understand the chemical contents of foods and normal medicines? After all the education, are they self-confident? Do our young adults understand and feel comfortable in their personal relationships? Have they a sense of responsibility and have they made a place for God in the centre of their lives; do they understand how to pray and pray often, and are they involved in caring for others?

4. Long-Term Future?

One practitioner in the field asked the question: "Must we not finally wonder, all things considered, assuming our child can read, write and do basic mathematics through teaching in the home, whether school, as we know it, will have any long-term future in this new epoch, our new society? Maybe our children in the foreseeable future, with their parents largely working from home, will be able to study, with their friends, all their normal subjects through the internet. The facility to communicate face to face through cyberspace is already in place. Included in the learning curve will be the setting up of contacts with students in other countries so that they will learn to converse and relate in numerous languages."

5. Back to Class in 2015

Teacher: "Take out your Economics books so today we can study supply and demand".

Student: "One moment please, teacher, our friend Sakimura is sending us a very important visual from Yokohama where they are testing their new solarcar invention that we feel could revolutionize travel."

Second Student: "It could be a great economic and ecological boon for us all if it is successful."

Third Student: "Some of us here in the class bought some shares in it last night on the globenet."

Fourth Student: "Also, Sir, we hope our investments will help pay for our up-coming trip to China."

Teacher: "No! Open your books at page twenty-three. I want no more interruptions. You can do what you want outside lesson time – but certainly not during my lesson period."

The bell rings, "……….. Sir, the test was successful, isn't that great… excuse us."

"Come on, let's hurry, it's time for the interactive meeting with our German friends…"

Yes, I have great hopes for our children.

References

1. www.colour-affects.co.uk/how.html

2. Forsythe, I. Jolliffe, A. and Stevens, D. (1995), *Delivering a Course*, London: Kogan Page Ltd.

3. Winch, C. and Gignell, J. (1999), *Key Concepts in the Philosophy of Education*, London: Routledge.

4. Cf. irlen.com/index.php; www.irlen.org.uk/Researchlist.htm

5. Gardner, H.(1993), *Multiple Intelligences*, New York: Basic Books. Hyland, A. (ed.) (2000), Multiple Intelligences, Cork (Ireland): Education Department, University College Cork.

6. Goleman, D. (2002), *The New Leaders*, London: Little, Brown. Cf. www. danielgoleman.info

7. McGeachy, C. (2001), *Spiritual Intelligence in the Workplace*, Dublin: Veritas.

8. Groome, T. (1998), *Educating for Life*, USA: Thomas Moore.

9. Warren, M. (1997), *Faith, Culture and the Worshipping Community*, New York: Paulist Press. (1998), *Youth Gospel Liberation*, Dublin: Veritas Publications.

10. Cole, B. (1993), *Music and Morals*, New York: Alba House.

11. Livingston, P. (1992), *Lessons of the Heart*, Indiana: Notre Dame Press. [P. 124]

About the Author

 Cormac O'Brolcháin, a Spiritan priest, having studied philosophy and psychology at U.C.D. (N.U.I.), and music at the Dublin College of Music, began his teaching career in the West Indies (1962-1965). On returning to Ireland, he continued his studies for four further years reading theology and music, during which time he was ordained to the priesthood (1968). In 1969 he was appointed to East Africa. After a year in parish work, he spent thirteen years as teacher, Principal and then Headmaster of St. Mary's School, Nairobi. In 1984 he was awarded an M.Litt (T.C.D.) for his evaluative research on the experimental use of music, para-liturgies and drama in religious education. Three years after returning to Ireland (1984), he was appointed Principal of Blackrock College, Dublin, (1987). He retired as Principal in 2000. In 2002 he was awarded a Ph.D., (D.C.U.), for his research into the importance of experiential religious education in the religious development of adolescent boys. In 2005, after three years as Chaplain in Willow Park School, he was appointed President of Blackrock College, Dublin.